Devon's Seaside History

Paul White

Bossiney Books

Children's bathing costumes, 1920
The cover photograph is of Sidmouth and the title page
photograph is of Burgh Island

First published 2019 by
Bossiney Books Ltd, 67 West Busk Lane, Otley, LS21 3LY
www.bossineybooks.com
© 2019 Paul White   All rights reserved
ISBN 978-1-906474-73-7

Acknowledgements

The picture on page 8 is an original watercolour from Walker's
The Costume of Yorkshire, reproduced by kind permission of the
Yorkshire Archaeological & Historical Society. The photographs on
page 27 are by kind permission of Kirsty McHugh. All other illustrations
are from the author's and publisher's own collections.

Printed in Great Britain by R Booth Ltd, Penryn, Cornwall

Introduction

Before the middle of the eighteenth century, the seaside as we understand it did not exist, in Devon or elsewhere. Visitors to Devon such as Celia Fiennes (1695) or Daniel Defoe (1724) are interested in ports as centres of trade, but they make no effort to describe, or even visit, the coast. Defoe, for example, writes

> A little to the southward of [Dartmouth], and to the east of the port, is Torbay, of which I know nothing proper to my observation, more than that it is a very good road for ships...

The ports and harbours were mostly inland, on the navigable rivers. The coastline itself had a number of tiny fishing communities, but even here many fishermen were only part-time, also working on farms. Much of Devon's fishing industry in the eighteenth century involved seasonal work across the Atlantic in Newfoundland, rather than coastal fishing.

But in 1750 Dr Richard Pococke, an Englishman who held Irish bishoprics but seems to have spent most of his time travelling, wrote:

> I went on to Star Cross, and crossed over the river to Exmouth, situated near the place where the Ex [sic] empties itself into the sea, and is chiefly inhabited by fishermen and publicans, it being a place to which the people of Exeter much resort for diversion and bathing in the sea, and the situation is so pleasant, having beautiful little hills to the east finely improved, and a view of the fine country on the other side, that some persons of condition have come to live at the place, which they are improving by a gravel walk to the river, that is to be planted, and they are going to make a bowling green.

So here are two groups of people turning Exmouth into a seaside town, 'the people of Exeter' and 'some persons of condition'. Quite what is meant by 'the people of Exeter' is unclear – merchants, lawyers and their families? Or apprentice lads and their girlfriends?

The transition to 'seaside' – the development of coastal towns designed to cater for visitors, followed by the broader spread of tourism in the twentieth century which is the subject of this book – has three persistent themes: leisure, health benefits, and access.

Wear · M.ʳ Fidsleigh · West Teignmouth · Won Cliff · East Teignmouth

nton · Wear · M.ʳ Bampfield · Teign · River · Billy · Ruins of a Fort

Comb Cellars · St Nicholas · Ringmore · A Bar Harbour

kland · Parsonage · Teignharvey · Shaldon · Ness Point

enry Gould · Crofs · Comb in Teign-head · Netherton

ay · Comb in Teign-head · Stoke in Teign-head

Ilber Down · Haccomb Chappel & Seat · Jobbers Crofs

Aller M.ʳ Bayley · Lady Caren

ORD HUND.ᴰ

Lower Cable · Cable · M. 3. 30. S.

Kings-Kerfwell · Daccomb Hamlet

Coffinfwell

er Hamlet · K. 3. 4 M. · Barton

TOR · Edginfwell Hamlet · Comb Pafsords Babicomb · Babicomb Bay

K. 3. 4. 2. C. · Shiphay · Witson Esq. · Mary Church

vton · Kents Hole · Anftis Cove · HOPE'S NOSE

Tor Mohun · Tor Wood · Donnegal Hilsen · Lead Stone or Flat-Rock

Mallock Esq. · Tor Abby Cary Esq.ʳ · Tor Quay · M.ʳ Elford · Hope

Cockington · Ore Stone

Shag or White Rock · Thatcher

Five Lanes · T. 11. 6. S.

Smoaky House

K. 35. P. · D · TOR

Preston

P. 2. 4. 4. C.

Torbay Althouse · Payngton Head · BAY

Payngton · Roundham Red Cliff

K. K. 13. 4. 30. D.

Goderington

C. 4. 0. 20. P.

Broad Sand

ton · Watton Rogers Esq.ʳ · Sharpstone Point

Court Yard Esq. · Brixham Quay · Ruins of · BERRY HEAD

Leisure

In the eighteenth century and for most of the nineteenth, society was rigidly divided between 'working people' and 'the leisured classes'. By definition a genteel person could not be involved in trade – in theory at least: there were of course dukes who spent time thinking about 'improving' their land or exploiting it by coal mines, but they had agents to carry out the managerial work. Family historians may discover in the Victorian censuses an ancestor who has been in trade but whose occupation suddenly becomes 'gentleman' once they retire.

The 'working people' included a minority who were merchants or manufacturers, and who might well be richer than the idle gentry around them, but were looked down on; to describe them historians often use the term 'the middling sort', not wishing to use the term 'middle class' in case it carries anachronistic connotations.

Such people might spend considerable amounts of money and as much time as they could spare on leisure activities, often with their family: in many cases their aim was to cease working, acquire a country estate, and become gentry.

The majority of the population had few resources and little time for leisure – though surprisingly, in the eighteenth century they had more days of leisure than in the nineteenth: however, they would not be paid for any time they took off. As well as Sundays, there were many traditional local holidays – saints' days ('holy days') and the days of local fairs – and then there was also the tradition jokingly known as 'St Monday': it was quite normal for working people to take Monday off if they chose to do so, and perhaps the fact that our Bank Holidays occur on Mondays is a relic of that.

But all that changed: a factory or even a bank could not operate efficiently if it didn't know whether its workers would show up after their Sunday off. By 1800 Monday was a normal working day, and in general employers were cutting down on time allowed off. The Bank of England itself had 47 full days of holiday in 1750, 18 by 1830, and just 4 by 1834. Scrooge appeared to have triumphed.

Yet, as we shall see later in the book, through the nineteenth century the total number of hours worked weekly tended to decrease, and paid

Torbay and Teignmouth in 1765, showing how little development had occurred. No wonder Defoe knew 'nothing proper to my observation'

holidays were gradually introduced, though initially only for white-collar workers.

By contrast, the majority of the leisured classes were indeed permanently at leisure, and they sought ways to keep themselves amused, first and foremost by socialising. Just as London had its 'season', so there were 'seasons' for visiting spa towns such as Bath, Tunbridge Wells or Scarborough: one member of a family might have an illness, but the whole family accompanied them to the spa for the season.

In the second half of the eighteenth century seaside towns began to compete with the spas. As William Cowper put it in 1781:

> Your prudent grandmammas, ye modern belles,
> Content with Bristol, Bath and Tunbridge Wells,
> When health required it would consent to roam,
> Else more attach'd to pleasures found at home.
> But now alike, gay widow, virgin, wife
> Ingenious to diversify dull life,
> In coaches, chaises, caravans and hoys,
> Fly to the coast for daily, nightly joys,
> And impatient of dry land, agree
> With one consent to rush into the sea.

The seaside for health

In 1753 Dr Richard Russell published *A dissertation concerning the use of sea water in diseases of the glands* in which he stated:

> … beyond all doubt salts have a great share in the cures done by medicinal waters. They are to be found in Bath waters, as Dr Guidot's experiments shew; and Dr Seip found a large quantity of white, bitter salt, in the Pyrmont waters.
>
> These, and the many other qualities, which evidently appear in sea water, may very justly raise in us the greatest hopes and expectations, that from this part of nature also some signal advantages may arise, to the practice of physic, and the general good of mankind…
>
> [Sea bathing places] should be clean and neat, at some distance from the opening of a river; that the water may be as highly loaded with sea salt, and the other riches of the ocean, as possible, and not weakened by the mixing of fresh water with its waves. In the next place, one would choose the shore

to be sandy and flat; for the conveniency of going into the sea in a bathing chariot. And lastly, that the sea shore should be bounded by lively cliffs and downs; to add to the cheerfulness of the place, and give the person that has bathed an opportunity of mounting on horseback dry and clean; to pursue such exercises as may be advised by his physician, after he comes out of the bath.

The initial idea was that drinking seawater would be good for health, but soon bathing was also recommended. Bathing, however, did not mean swimming, and it certainly was not meant to be pleasurable. The patient would normally be 'dipped' by two muscular attendants (male or female as appropriate) and it should be done early in the morning, so that there would be a cold shock.

A third health benefit soon entered the picture: fresh sea air. TB, known as 'consumption', was prevalent among all classes, and spending the winter in the South of France was widely recommended for those who could afford it; but soon after the French Revolution, travel to the Continent became dangerous. Mild sea air was now the answer, and the Devon coast in winter was much favoured, particularly Torquay.

Doctors were also becoming aware of other factors, including the psychological. Dr A P Buchan in 1804 wrote:

> In that state of society, when the general diffusion of wealth has removed from a considerable part of the community all apprehensions respecting the immediate means of subsistence, the mind, not being engaged in providing against real wants, is obliged to find employment in the creation of such as are imaginary…
>
> The pursuit of health, of which the importance is universally acknowledged, forms to the rich an apology for that frequent change of place which, in reality, originates in a hope of finding, in some new situation, objects to excite the attention, and occupy that intellectual vacuity, the perception of which constitutes the chief misery of the idle.

Poor old leisured classes! But there was more to it than hypochondria: overcrowding in cities, or even permanent residence there, really was bad for your health. A change of scene and a change of routine were

A bathing machine on the Yorkshire coast. Being 'dipped' was a medical treatment, not a pleasure

good for you:

> At present the tide of fashion carries those who want, or think they want, health, towards the sea. Nor does any situation seem better calculated to promote the well-being of either the real, or the imaginary valetudinarian. The view of the wide expanded ocean, in its ever varying forms, elevates and exhilarates the mind, while the cool and vivifying breezes, which play round its shores, ventilate the withered lungs, and dispel that languor of mind, and lassitude of limbs, which are but too familiar to those who are obliged to pass the sultry months of summer in a great city…

The language is dated, but the observation is surely still true. Dr Buchan was a scientist, and promoted research into such things. He even conducted experiments on himself, not always successfully, as when he tried to take his temperature when shivering after coming out of the sea, and his teeth cracked the thermometer.

The Devon seaside, 1750-1815

The earliest genteel seaside watering places (in the world, not just in Britain) seem to have been spas where the mineral spring was near the sea, at the foot of the cliffs at Whitby ('What the drinking cannot purge away is cured with ease by dipping in the sea,' 1718) and at Scarborough ('It is the custom here for not only the gentlemen, but also the ladies, to bathe in the sea,' 1732), both in Yorkshire. Before long Margate, Brighton and other south coast resorts were also being mentioned.

How did this affect Devon? Initially, very little, and the reason was access. The county was very poorly connected. When Thomas Curwen arrived in Exeter in 1776, he had taken 17 hours to get from Bristol (averaging 5 mph), and was told that coaches had been unknown in the city 40 years previously. In much of Devon wheeled transport was still rare in 1800. Curwen was an American in exile, a royalist refugee, and he had not been able to bring all his fortune with him. He found Sidmouth ideal because it was cheap. 'This watering place, the resort of much genteel company for sea bathing, is the most frugal place in England.' He was less keen on Exmouth (within the parish of Withycombe Raleigh) but his comments help us understand those of Dr Pococke 26 years previously:

> Afternoon at Withycomb-Raleigh parish, lying at the mouth of the river Exe; the houses are chiefly low, with mud walls and thatched roofs; though there are a considerable number of brick, covered with slate, reputable and handsome, owned chiefly by Exeter people, who come down in shoals on Saturday afternoons for the purpose of pastime and festivity among themselves on Sundays; this being almost the only resort on that day, when the town is full of them, not, as I am told, to the emolument or wish of the inhabitants.
>
> Drank tea at Mr E. per invitation and walkt [sic] with young ladies on Shephards Walk amidst shoals of Exeter damsels whose insufferable undress and ill breeding justly exposes them to the contempt and derision of strangers...

Exmouth was exceptional within Devon in being accessible from a city with a large population. At that time Exeter was still wealthy from the cloth trade, which would soon begin to suffer from northern

Sidmouth around 1830. Compare this with the cover photograph

competition. The new brick houses in Exmouth were in many cases owned by Exeter people, and the locals Curwen knew didn't like that. The problem of second-home owners, making a brief appearance and not spending much locally, has already appeared!

Sidmouth was particularly successful at this time, and it retains a great deal of its late Georgian architecture. By 1788 The Rev S Shaw proclaimed it 'much frequented in the bathing season, and many families continue their residence even during the winter.' Fanny Burney, visiting in 1791, said of Sidmouth

> … the terrace for company is nearer to the ocean than any I have elsewhere seen, & therefore both more pleasant & more commodious. The little bay is of a most peaceful kind, & the sea was as calm & gentle as the Thames. I longed to bathe, but I am in no state now to take liberties with myself, &, having no advice at hand, I ran no risk.

Like its local rivals, Sidmouth would gain greatly when the French Revolution and wars made continental travel dangerous. It gained even more from a brief visit by King George III in 1790. The Devon historian Richard Polwhele in 1793 said it was:

much frequented by people of fashion – near three hundred yearly; and there is a constant succession of company. With respect to their accomodation, Sidmouth can boast an elegant ball-room, and on the beach, a commodious tea-room and shed, frequented by Ladies as well as Gentlemen... But Sidmouth is not esteemed merely as the resort of people whose pursuit is pleasure. It is very commonly recommended to invalids, particularly to those who are affected by consumptions, as many of the faculty think this situation equal to the south of France.

Two years later John Swete said:

Sidmouth is the gayest place of resort on the Devon coast, and every elegancy, every luxury, every amusement is here to be met with — iced creams, milliners' shops, cards, billiards, plays, circulation libraries, attract notice in every part.

Circulating libraries provided their subscribing members with books to borrow, ranging from frivolous novels to academic works, a reading room with magazines and newspapers, a souvenir gift shop and above all facilities for socialising. Theatres appeared, but were a failure – the audiences too small. But the seaside had natural advantages over the spas, including the beach for collecting shells, seaweeds and fossils. Hot sea water baths could be provided, making cold dippings unnecessary. There could be boat trips, and annual regattas from as early as 1775 (Starcross). These events grew bigger as the years passed.

Teignmouth and Dawlish were also by this time catering for the genteel market, but because of poor access, most of their visitors were Devon gentry, or gentry from further afield seeking cheap accommodation in the short term, or for retirement, particularly officers from the navy and the East India Company.

Among the visitors were Jane Austen's family, once her father had retired to Bath. Their first known visit was in 1801, when they spent three months in Sidmouth. The following year they were in Dawlish but presumably did not enjoy it (Jane was subsequently scathing about the quality of the circulating library) because they soon transferred to Teignmouth.

The north Devon coast was slower to develop, partly because the

This just might be the building Jane Austen stayed in at Teignmouth!

south was generally warmer, but mainly because access was even more difficult. However in 1800 Rev Richard Warner of Bath reported of Ilfracombe:

> A number of good houses, chiefly for the accommodation of strangers in the summer season, range along the side of this harbour, and the remainder of the town stretches for a mile in length to the westward of it. A pebbly shore in the same direction, with some good machines, afford convenient bathing.

North Devon was 'only accessible by the worst roads in the kingdom' according to T H Williams in *Picturesque Excursions in Devonshire* (1804). The coach from Tiverton to Barnstaple averaged just 2 mph. The north coast could of course be accessed by sea, but in the days of sail this was unreliable – you might be trapped there by a contrary wind – and few visitors chose to do so.

If Ilfracombe was hard to reach, Lynton and Lynmouth were even more so, being ten miles from the nearest road, but they were becoming famous for their scenic qualities. Whereas places along the south coast were 'picturesque', the north was both picturesque and 'sublime' – which meant pleasurably scary.

The Valley of Rocks as 'seen' by early tourists, and (below) as seen today

Lynmouth, an illustration from about 1830

Young people who would in the past have crossed the Alps on their way to Italy now visited Lynton on foot for its aesthetic quality, often seeing themselves as explorers. In 1789 John Swete noted 'With such a scene before me, how poor in comparison seemed the gaieties of the town.' William Wordsworth in 1797, staying in the Quantock hills, wrote:

> Coleridge, my sister and myself started from Alfoxden with a view to visit Lynton and the Valley of the Stones... In the course of this walk was planned the poem of the Ancient Mariner.

They repeated the walk several times, as did Southey in 1799 and Shelley in 1812. There was scarcely any accommodation in Lynton until an inn was opened in 1800 and the Valley of Rocks hotel in 1807, but, as one author wrote, 'even the ardent lover of the sublime and the beautiful would not remain longer than a day' because of 'the absence of social intercourse'.

The pre-Victorian period

When the Napoleonic wars ended in 1815 and the continent was once more accessible, Devon resorts suffered – all the more so because they were largely dependent on local gentry and merchants who were going through hard times. Corn prices were low so that landowners as well as farmers suffered, and the extensive Devon cloth trade was shrinking rapidly.

The one exception to the decline of the resorts was Torquay, which was a winter rather than a summer resort, and retained its reputation as a place for invalids. In 1841 Dr Augustus Bozzi published *The Spas of England and Principal Sea Bathing Places*, in which he says 'No sea nook has been been more talked of in this country, for the last fifteen or twenty years, than Torquay... the south-western asylum of condemned lungs'.

He visited the town and was much impressed that 'a good assemblage of white or stone-coloured gay-looking houses, around a still harbour, unruffled by wind, was even more calculated to produce cheering and salutary impressions.' Doctors had no cure for TB, but they were aware of the importance of optimism for human health. Bozzi found that his hotel had a 'spitting pot' in every room. There was coughing from the neighbouring rooms.

The harbourside was well protected from the gale that was blowing, but there was little choice of where to walk: the strand was

> filled in general with respirator-bearing people, who look like muzzled ghosts, and are ugly enough to frighten the younger people to death... If Messrs. Carey and Shedden would permit a level road to be made under the rock by the Abbey Torr, Torquay would be delightfully improved.

That road was built just a year later, part of a massive investment in infrastructure. A new harbour was opened in 1807, a road was engineered from Torquay to Kingsteignton and another from the new Shaldon Bridge.

At the same time, housing was developed for genteeel residents, and the hillsides above the harbour retain a superb collection of villa architecture from the period.

Bozzi remarks that 'house-rent during the season, which begins in September, and extends generally a great way into the month of May,

Early Victorian prints of Torquay (above) and Ilfracombe (below).

Once the railway arrived in Torquay there were merchants who wanted to enlarge the harbour as a commercial port – but were voted down

will be anything but reasonable.' A terrace house with two good bedrooms would be 5 guineas a week, a detached villa 10 to 13 guineas, hugely expensive at the time. Torquay was aiming at the wealthy classes, as indeed were all the other south coast resorts, though for a time the other resorts were increasingly dependent on new residents rather than holidaymakers.

The Victorian period

Transport infrastructure had a huge influence on seaside development, and nowhere more so than in Devon. By 1822 there were steamer services to Ilfracombe from Bristol and Swansea, and they were relatively cheap. Passengers could also stop off at Lynmouth, but they had to be carried ashore in small boats. Steamers were the initial reason for the building of seaside piers, making landing passengers easy.

And North Devon suddenly acquired usable roads – that from Exeter to Barnstaple in 1830 being the most important, with extensions both to Ilfracombe and Bideford. With these new connections in place, Ilfracombe started to develop in the way the southern resorts had done forty years earlier, with assembly rooms, three competing circulating libraries and tunnels through the cliff to the beach. For a short time Ilfracombe, and to a lesser extent Instow and Lynton, had an advantage over the south coast, but it was not to last long.

The next transport revolution, the railway, all but defined the Victorian age, making travel faster, cheaper and much more comfortable. Devon was suddenly accessible from London or Birmingham – though the initial rationale for most lines was freight rather than passengers, certainly not seasonal passengers. The railways even at their peak did not reach all parts of Devon, and during the Victorian period some resorts benefited greatly, while others suffered from comparative remoteness.

The GWR main line from Bristol reached Exeter in 1844. Trains from London took $4^{1}/_{2}$ hours, averaging 43 mph, then the fastest train service in the world. By 1846 there was a line to Dawlish and Teignmouth, and by 1848 to Torre on the outskirts of Torquay. There were direct services to these resorts from London, Birmingham and south Wales.

Even when the LSWR line to Exeter was completed, with branches to Exmouth (1861), Seaton (1868) and Sidmouth (1874), passengers had to make at least one change. GWR resorts had a huge advantage over LSWR resorts.

In the north, the line to Barnstaple (1854) was of limited use for tourism. Ilfracombe was not connected until 1874, Lynton 1898, Appledore 1908. By that time railways were obsolescent: the Westward Ho! and Appledore line closed in 1917.

For the south coast resorts, however, the railways were a godsend – provided they wanted lots of visitors. But did they? By the 1860s many white-collar workers were given a fortnight's paid holiday. By the 1890s there were direct trains bringing the working classes from as far away as Liverpool. Tensions arose within many towns, with residents (and some posh hotel owners) wanting just elite visitors, whilst other businesses were keen for ever greater numbers.

The results were very varied. At Clovelly the Lords of the Manor would allow no development. At Sidmouth there was no railway link until 1874, by which time the demand was for sandy beaches which Sidmouth lacked: the town went into a doze for the rest of the century – but both Clovelly and Sidmouth would later benefit from the lack of Victorian development. At Dawlish the railway was a mixed blessing, as it cut the resort off from its beach. Teignmouth seized the opportunity to develop its docks, which already shipped ball clay and granite. (Some Torquay entrepreneurs wanted to do likewise, but were voted down.)

When a resort wanted to attract holidaymakers, what did it need to do? An attractive promenade had always been essential, but the addition of gardens where visitors could stroll and facilities such as tennis courts were an attraction. Westward Ho! was planned as an entirely new exclusive resort, featuring the first golf club founded by English players, in 1866 – and two years later the first ladies golf club in Britain – but it never achieved the financial success its founders had hoped for. (Charles Kingsley, whose novel gave its name to Westward Ho!, was horrified by what had happened to the Burrows.)

At many resorts elegant entertainments were provided, including concerts in the traditional assembly rooms or elsewhere. Torquay even had its own orchestra.

The naturalist Philip Gosse of St Marychurch was a keen observer of marine biology: his 1854 book *The Aquarium* (he had invented the word) started a craze for collecting both seaweeds and animals, using

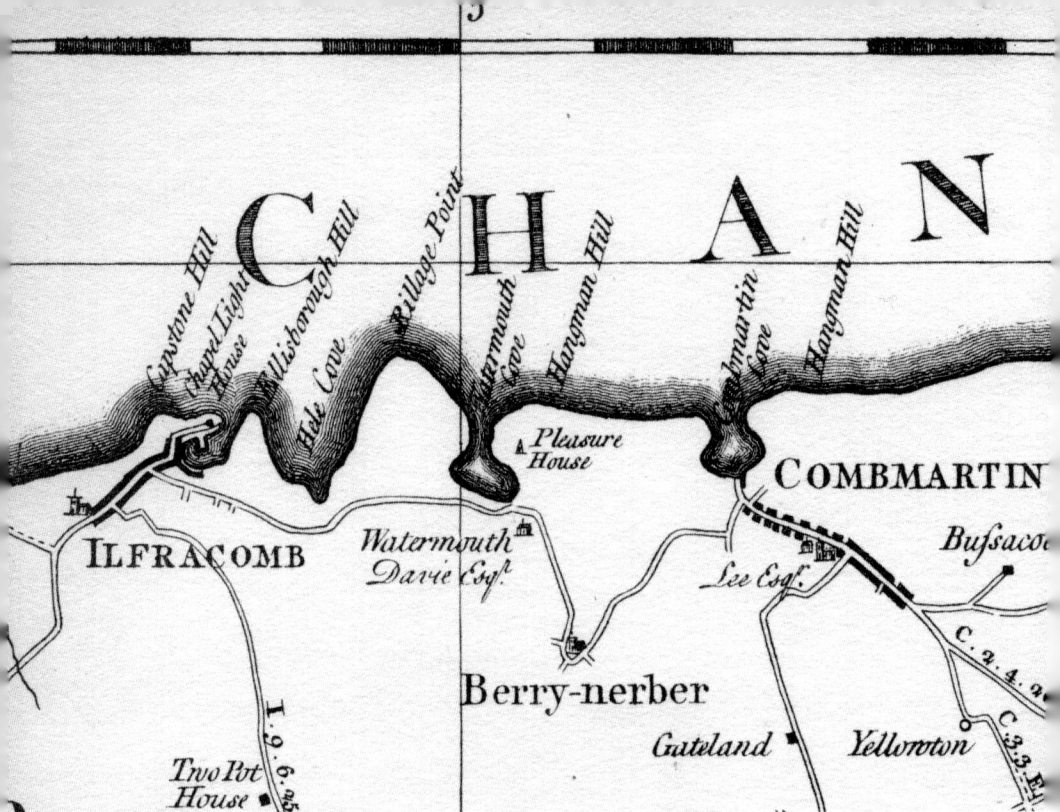

CHAN

Capstone Hill
Chapel Light House
Hillisborough Hill
Hele Cove
Rillage Point
Watermouth Cove
Hangman Hill
Combmartin Cove
Hangman Hill

Pleasure House

COMBMARTIN

ILFRACOMB

Watermouth
Davie Esq.

Lee Esq.

Bufsaco

Berry-nerber

Gateland   Yellowton

Two Pot House

Ilfracombe in 1765

nets, geologists' hammers, dredging and even trawling; far more people took it up than he had expected, and before long all the rock-pools of Torbay and Ilfracombe had been ransacked. Self-education during their holiday appealed to a large serious-minded section of the middle classes, and in 1856 Charlotte Chanter (Charles Kingsley's sister) wrote *Ferny Combes* which inspired visitors to do similar havoc to rare Devon fern species.

Beach access was always important, and sometimes required both investment and ingenuity. At Ilfracombe tunnels were dug through the cliffs, to create separate bathing areas and pools for gentlemen and ladies. Similar efforts were needed at Plymouth, which is often ignored by seaside historians because it was not primarily a resort, but it attracted large numbers of genteel visitors, not least naval officers' families.

As the century progressed, Paignton's splendid beach became ever more attractive to visitors, but it was separated from the village by a

At Dawlish the railway was a mixed blessing, since it cut the town off from its beach

marsh. So the marsh was drained and much of the modern town dates from the period 1875-1890.

Sandy beaches had become increasingly attractive because people now actively wanted to swim in the sea, rather than being 'dipped' for their health. By the end of the century, the seaside was a place for family holidays: the era of the bucket and spade had begun.

There were now too many visitors for them to be forced into bathing machines, which created problems, especially in prudish Victorian England. The first was that 'morality' required that men and women should bathe separately: most resorts assigned different sections of beach – though there might be mixed bathing areas for those prepared to walk a bit further. The second was that men had been used to bathe nude, and women in loose petticoats. Neither was acceptable in the new climate of opinion, and in most resorts there were strict rules. The Rev Francis Kilvert wrote in his diary in 1874:

> At Seaton while Dora was sitting on the beach I had a bathe. A boy brought me to the machine door two towels as I

Paignton pier, opened in 1879, originally had a theatre pavilion at the far end, but that was destroyed in a fire in 1919

thought, but when I came out of the water and began to use them I found that one of the rags he had given me was a pair of very short red and white striped drawers to cover my nakedness. Unaccustomed to such things and customs I had in my ignorance bathed naked and set at nought the conventions of the place and scandalized the beach. However some little boys who were looking on at the rude naked man appeared to be much interested in the spectacle, and the young ladies who were strolling near seemed to have no objection.

In practice the rules the rules usually weren't enforced. As the *Pall Mall Gazette* observed in 1866:

At every seaside resort there is to be found a class of visitors of both sexes of whose presence and custom the tradespeople and lodging house keepers are unwilling to be deprived, who derive a prurient gratification and employment in gazing on the naked and half naked forms of the bathers.

High tide was always a popular time on the promenade. 'Ladies out-raged decorum by viewing from the pier and the beach, through opera glasses, the antics of nude gentlemen.' This behaviour is not what we expect of Victorian England, where even the table legs (according to mythology) were expected to be veiled, but is perhaps indicative of a more general mood, that the seaside is a place where you can be free, unbuttoned even in the most literal sense.

By the 1880s a new moral attitude was demanding mixed bathing. Families mattered: they must not be separated by these old-fashioned ideas. Paignton, Dawlish and Torquay all reintroduced mixed bathing between 1896 and 1900, though neck to knee costumes were obliga-tory for both sexes.

A guide to Teignmouth in 1914 states that 'Visitors may bathe from the sand up to eight o'clock in the morning, after which they must use machines or tents.' At Sidmouth changing on the beach was prohib-ited until after 1945.

Excursionists

Most Devon resorts remained decidedly genteel. There was for most of the nineteenth century nothing to compare with Brighton, Margate or Blackpool, where vast numbers of day trippers from the big cities appeared at weekends, and the resorts grew at a great pace.

But in Ilfracombe it was rather different, because steamers brought excursionists from south Wales, where coal-fuelled industry was booming. The gentry of Lynton and Lynmouth prevented a pier being built there precisely to discourage such excursions.

Excursionists were mostly less affluent than other visitors, they had already spent a lot on their tickets, and they wanted to make the most of a rare opportunity for a day out: a Sunday Closing Act had made alcohol unavailable in Wales on the one day in the week which work-ers had off, but it was available on board the steamers. In 1877 400 excursionists arrived already drunk, and rampaged through the town attacking publicans and market people.

There were only twenty or so excursion trips each year, and not all were as disastrous, but the wealthy now avoided Ilfracombe in the summer: the town responded by banning steamers and trains on Sundays, but Saturdays and bank holidays remained boisterous. On August Bank Holiday in 1893 5500 excursionists arrived – nothing

Above: This couple from about 1930 suggest that not all working class excursionists were out for a wild time!

Right: An advertisement from 1914 for a hotel in Lynmouth. The building was damaged beyond repair in the 1952 flood

LYNMOUTH, NORTH DEVON.

LYNDALE HOTEL

The Oldest Established First-class Family Hotel in Lynmouth.

Nearest Hotel to Watersmeet, Doone Valley, and Most Central for Devon & Somerset Staghounds.

CHARGES STRICTLY MODERATE.
Electric Light Throughout.
HEADQUARTERS A. A.
Garage for 10 Cars adjoining Hotel. Petrol.
SALMON & TROUT FISHING.
Ilfracombe and Minehead Coaches stop at Hotel.
Conveyances meet all Trains.
GOOD STABLING.

Tel. 45
Lynton Exchange.
Telegrams—"LYNDALE, LYNMOUTH."
A. W. GAYDON, Proprietress.

compared to Blackpool or even Weston-super-Mare, of course – and even Exmouth had 3000 from Exeter.

By the 1890s Torquay had day excursion trains arriving from Bristol, Wolverhampton and London, but these seem never to have created the same problems. Torquay's advertising perhaps made it clear that it was not the kind of place to go for a rave, and the cost of travel was too high for many working class people. These visitors were more sedate.

The shingle beaches of east Devon meant that Seaton, Sidmouth and Budleigh Salterton saw very few excursionists.

Beaches such as this at Bantham, with Bigbury and Burgh Island beyond, were out of reach before motor transport, but would in any case have been little appreciated before sun-bathing became fashionable

Sun, sea and lots of sand

Towards the end of the century visitors' expectations were changing. Instead of the increasingly crowded resorts with their sociability and entertainments (whether genteel or otherwise) more people wanted a family holiday with their children. Building sand-castles was not new – an illustration appears in print as early as 1838 – but the beach holiday was to become increasingly popular. Paignton was the main beneficiary, expanding rapidly from 1870 onward.

However, the resort beaches, even where they weren't segregated, were often very crowded, whilst many of Devon's finest and largest beaches were inaccessible to most people, who depended on railways.

There were some signs of change. By 1891 Woolacombe was beginning to develop, two steep miles from Mortehoe Station: the hotel was employing a cook, two housemaids and a gardener and there were also two lodging houses. In the same year the Saunton Hotel

A charabanc in the early 1920s. Local coach companies enabled visitors staying in a resort to reach more distant beaches, and also to explore areas inland from the resort

was also open, probably on the site of the later Saunton Sands Hotel about three miles from Braunton Station, with the publisher's great-grandmother as its barmaid, but development would be slow – and on the south coast from Dartmouth to Plymouth, which railways would never reach, there was virtually no sign of the holiday industry. Even in 1911, Bigbury-on-Sea had just one lodging house and a tearoom, though there were a number of retired people living there.

This all changed rapidly after WW1 with the arrival of motor transport, both charabancs and, more importantly for Devon, private cars. Suddenly it was possible, if you were rich enough, to reach the wonderful secluded coves and beaches we now take for granted, though most people still stayed at hotels or guest houses in the resorts. Local charabanc companies provided excursions taking visitors staying in the resorts to beaches further afield.

From around 1920, but especially in the 1930s, the beaches were in even more demand for sun-bathing. In Victorian times genteel people avoided the sun: ladies thought it might damage their delicate complexions, but above all sunburn had been seen as an indicator of class. One wouldn't wish to be thought an agricultural labourer, would one? But when most labourers spent twelve hours a day in a factory, and

Woolacombe beach, 9 September 1936. Seaside holidays were perhaps more sociable then: many of this group, previously unknown to each other, were staying at the same Ilfracombe guest house and went on a coach excursion together

only the super-rich could afford the time and money to head for the sunshine, that changed. A tan became not only a sign of wealth, but also of health, especially when pallid TB faces were all too common. The connection with skin cancer was as yet unsuspected.

Before long improved roads to the new beaches led to a demand for parking, and other facilities such as shops and cafés soon appeared, which in some cases destroyed the original atmosphere.

By the 1930s car ownership was growing. Even the author's father, son of a London dock worker, had a car in 1936 and twice stayed at Ilfracombe, using it as a base to make forays into Cornwall as well as Exmoor. (The car proved expensive to maintain: he had to sell it.)

Camping was becoming popular. More and more workers received a decent amount of paid holiday, and subsequent decades saw holiday camp sites with chalets or static caravans: between 1950 and 1980 the number of self-catering visitors at Dawlish Warren increased from 500 to 10,000. There was then a huge rise in towed caravans from the

Camping, in various forms, was cheaper than staying in guest houses or hotels

The motor car made parts of Devon accessible to families for the first time. This is a Scottish family who had driven from Ayrshire, seen here at Clovelly

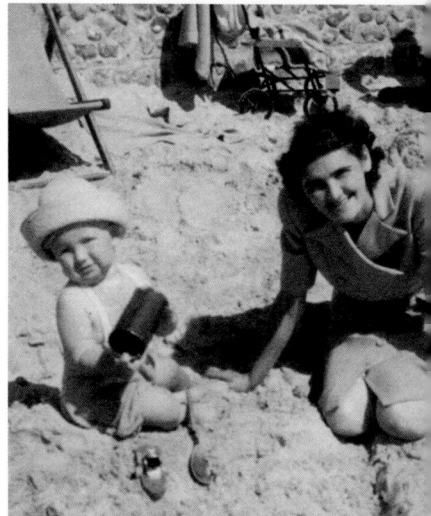

1960s, as well as camper vans – many of them produced in Devon: a Sidmouth company started in 1956 was selling 3500 VW camper van conversions a year at its peak.

This was followed by a growth in self-catering in 'holiday cottages' which were often converted farm buildings.

The narrowly resort-based seaside was a thing of the past, and the various resorts themselves developed differently – not least due to the two world wars. Cinemas and amusement arcades appeared, and at Plymouth the art deco Tinside Pool.

*Opposite:
The classic
beach holiday,
around 1950*

*Right: Today's
visitors to
Devon are
able to enjoy
a huge variety
of experiences,
from the views
of Lynton which
excited the
Romantic poets
to the delights
of Brixham –
but even this
is not new:
Murray's 1872
Handbook had
said 'Every
intelligent
traveller
will visit
[Brixham], as
it is unique of
its kind'*

During the inter-war years, and even until the mid-1950s, Torquay continued to regard itself as competing with the French Riviera rather than with other British resorts, and the local authority spent a great deal on advertising and other facilities to support tourism, including the purchase of the Cockington estate in 1932.

The effects of the world wars

In Devon as everywhere else both wars had a huge impact on those individuals who lost close family members, but the economic effects were varied. Ilfracombe was among the worst hit by WW1, since the excursions stopped immediately. Almost 30% of the town's dwellings were boarding houses or hotels, and many of them were bankrupted. After WW1 there was a brief revival, but then coal strikes and the terrible effects of the depression in South Wales were disastrous. At exactly the time when Ilfracombe most needed its railway links, the Southern Railway cut back, even removing Sunday services. The brutal truth was that railway companies could not run a year-round seven-day-a-week service for tourists arriving only at the weekends in summer.

When the Second World War began, Ilfracombe had not recovered from the First, though its accommodation facilities were extensively used by the military and for evacuees. After the war, petrol rationing had a devastating effect: wealthy private motorists did not have the fuel to get there. By contrast the railway brought 10,000 visitors each Saturday: it was a boom time in numbers if not in wealth. But the arrival of foreign package holidays had a severe impact on that market too. The railway closed in 1970, the last steamer service in 1972.

All of which sounds very depressing, but Ilfracombe remains the lively centre of an extraordinarily attractive area, and with an economy now partly based on light engineering it is much less dependent than it once was on providing accommodation for tourists – which paradoxically makes it more attractive.

Teignmouth was another major sufferer, being bombed 21 times between 1940 and 1944, with many dead and over 2000 houses damaged or destroyed as well as its hospital.

Torquay seems to have suffered less. In WW1 it hosted a number of military hospitals (at one of which Agatha Christie worked as a nurse then as a pharmacist) and was a 'staging area' where troops gathered before being shipped out. During WW2 it suffered some bombing, but mostly from planes with a bomb or two left after blitzing Plymouth. It was a gathering place for American troops heading for the D-Day landings.

Much of the coastline during the war was occupied by troops, often in camp-sites as at Croyde or Northam, or in the area near Slapton Sands where the entire population of 3000 people was evacuated to allow for the D-Day preparations – but that story has its own books to commemorate it.

Since 1945

Yet another transport revolution soon occurred, but unlike roads, railways and the motor car, this one had a negative effect on Devon tourism – the expansion of jet aviation. Firstly the jet-set began to fly to sunnier climes (long gone were the days when Torquay was a winter resort, thought too hot to be visited in summer) then came the rise of the package holiday.

Whilst some resorts did suffer in the short term, the increase in national wealth after 1950 meant that the total number of holidays taken rose, and the number taken within the UK did not fall – indeed the south-west's share of the UK visitor market increased. By 1978 Devon played host to 3.4 million tourists, most of them heading for the seaside – but perhaps fewer stayed in the traditional resorts, and in many cases just for a week, as a second holiday.

One reason for this was the huge rise in the number of cars, from 2.2 million in 1950 to 14 million by 1980: Devon is a county best explored by car. Whilst most visitors stayed near the coast, typical holidays for car owners would include trips to inland areas, especially Dartmoor and Exmoor, and trips to other parts of the Devon coast.

As ever more people became familiar with Devon, and felt themselves more secure when the economy improved after the war (despite hiccups), the county attracted retired people. This was not new: in 1911 when nationally just 7% of the population was over 60, it was 16% in Budleigh Salterton and over 12% in both Ilfracombe and Torquay – but during the 1960s and early 1970s East Devon in particular saw a large increase, resulting in low density suburban developments near the coast: nowadays 40% of Sidmouth's population is retired.

There is a far wider variety of experience in most modern 'seaside' holidays in Devon than would have been the case a century ago. Of course families with young children rightly spend a lot of time on the beach, and relatively remote but superb beaches such as Saunton, Blackpool Sands and Bantham are fully used, but at the same time activities such as walking the coast path, photography, interest in heritage, wildlife and geology have replaced the poolside deckchair.

And underlying this is a truth as powerful as it was more than two centuries ago, that 'The view of the wide expanded ocean, in its ever varying forms, elevates and exhilarates the mind...'

Slapton Sands

Some other Bossiney books which may interest you

Devon Beach and Cove Guide
Devon's Geology – an Introduction
Devon's Smugglers – the Truth behind the Fiction
Dartmouth – a Shortish Guide
Torbay – the Visible History
Walking the South Devon Coast in 1854

Walks books

Fairly Easy Walks in North Devon
Shortish Walks in North Devon

Really Short Walks – South Devon
Shortish Walks – the South Devon Coast
Shortish Walks – Torbay and Dartmouth

Really Short Walks – East Devon
Shortish Walks – East Devon Coast